RECOLLECTIONS PAISLEY

by DONALD MALCOLM

To: Gordon, Derek and Lesley

Fascinating scenes of the High Street continue to turn up. This one dates from sometime before 1906. The distinctive building on the right, looking as if it belongs in a fairy tale, was William Watson's butcher shop. Located on the corner of New Street it was demolished around 1906. The YMCA now occupies the site. Watson still has a shop a few yards away. The third building down from the turretted fantasy, with the twin chimney stacks, was the oldest house in Paisley. The lamp standard across the road, where the horse and cart are dallying, advertised the Globe Hotel.

First published in the United Kingdom, 1992, This edition printed 2001
By Stenlake Publishing, 54-58 Mill Square, Catrine, Ayrshire. KA5 6RD
Telephone/Fax: 01290 551122
e-mail: sales@stenlake.co.uk website: www.stenlake.co.uk

ISBN 1-840331-82-8

The Highland Show was held at Paisley Racecourse in July 1913. The *Gazette* of the 5th speculated as to why it was the first occasion the Show had been held in the town. 'In many things our town is really hampered by its proximity to a great city as Glasgow is ...' The Show opened on Tuesday the 8th. Activities included parades of prize cattle, jumping competitions and music provided from two bandstands. The wooden town of stables and offices required for what was 'likely to prove the best show ever held in the history of the Highland Society' covered 40 acres. Crudely produced cards are known from the show. Shown here is a superior production advertising Alex Cross & Sons, Cake Manufacturers, Glasgow.

INTRODUCTION

The aim of this book, as it was in *Yesterday's Paisley*,is to provide interest, variety and information in a way that will stimulate readers, no matter what their age, to look afresh at our town. Many favourable comments were received about the first volume and the content and style have been continued here. The book has gone into a reprint. My thanks, and those of my editor and friend, Richard Stenlake, to those discerning enough to stock or to purchase copies.

Some duplication of scenes with other publications is inevitable, but I have kept it to a minimum and tried to find new things to write about such cards. Hitherto unknown postcards are still turning up, so the theme is likely to remain fresh.

While, once again, I have had the good fortune to talk to friends and to strangers, who gave generously of their time and expertise, any errors are mine.

I think of my postcards as cardboard time machines. They take me back to my own past and to that of the town. Climb aboard and join me and I hope that you enjoy the trip!

Acknowledgements to Derek Malcolm (title and research); Ken Hinshalwood and the staff of the Local History Department, Renfrew District Libraries; David Norval (ex-organist of the Coats Memorial); Rev. D.G. Palmer; and to Bob Grieves, David Rowand and Frank Walker, for keeping me right on transport, the history of Paisley and architectural features respectively; Dr Sylvia Clark; Mrs Claire Baxter; Senior Library Supervisor, Local Studies, Paisley Central Library; Assistant Divisional Officer Patrick O'Hara, Strathclyde Fire Brigade; and finally, my very good friend, Peter Westwood, for the notes on the Burns cards and for his excellent drawing of Paisley Tramways map.

The Show was back in Paisley in June 1950. Apparently the show area covered about 60 acres, with an additional 45 acres for parking. 'Most of those who had taken ground space struck a bright note with their pavilions - without being garish - and it was a case of flowers, flowers everywhere, while flags, streamers and banners fluttered aloft' (*Gazette*, 24th June). Three hundred workmen were needed to put up the 25,000 feet of strand frontage, the 750,000 square feet of canvas and two miles of roads using 10,000 railway sleepers within the site.

This view looking east at the junction of Whitehaugh Avenue is substantially unchanged today, although there have been individual and collective alterations to parts of the row of fine houses on the left. The building on the extreme left is the Arthur Allison Memorial Hall. It now looks neglected and sorry for itself. In the distance is Barshaw Park.

Much of this scene has disappeared. Many of the houses on the left, the railway bridge and the steeple of Sherwood Church have all succumbed to the bulldozer. On the right lay the main Barracks and on the south side of the road, at Lacey Street, was the officers' quarters. The Barracks, known as Whitehaugh or Williamsburgh, were built as a result of the Radical troubles after the Napoleonic Wars and opened in 1820, one year after the Peterloo Massacre. The Barracks had virtually gone by 1947 and the Newfoundland Regiment was the last body of troops to be housed there.

This scene is late Victorian or early Edwardian. The structure in the centre of the square was provided as a shelter for the cabbies, by Mrs Arthur of Barshaw. Next to it is a horse drawn coach with a Lipton's Tea advert. There are no tram lines in evidence and the Post Office has still to get its extension.

Now the tram lines have appeared and the 1912 extension has been added to the Post Office. During the construction of the extension, the windows have become uniform in design and number and the tower, visible on the previous picture, has disappeared. The stonework containing the clock has also been re-designed. The road appears to have been widened also, presumably to facilitate the laying of the tram lines. This time, Lyon's Tea is getting some free advertising.

Since its foundation in 1163, when King David I's High Steward of Scotland appointed monks of the Cluniac Order to build a monastery on the White Cart, the Abbey has known turmoil and tranquility. Notably, with true Christian love, Edward I invoked the fire insurance policy in 1307. I don't think it matters that what we see today is virtually all restoration; it is the spirit that counts and the Abbey dreams on in all its timeless glory. Recently the expression 'down the drain' took on a whole new meaning when about 100 metres of the main drain of the Monastery was revealed (the Museum has produced an informative leaflet). These four cards show stages of the restoration from around 1902 till 1928 when the work was completed by Rowand Anderson.

To the north-east are the Gleniffer Braes and to the right of the Town Hall is the site of the, as yet unrestored, Abbey. Just look at all those chimneys - I counted at least forty! Imagine that lot submerging the Buddies in soot and fumes. The Saucel Brewery & Distillery is in the foreground. The distillery was founded in the 1790s and went bust around 1820 with debts of almost £9000. The site was near to the Glasgow, Paisley and Johnstone Canal and the Espedair Burn ran through the works.

The Society of the Sisters Faithful Companions of Jesus was founded in Amiens in 1820. St. Margaret's Convent School (for boarding and day pupils) was established as the result of a bequest to staff at St. Catherine's School and the Sisters took possession in February 1889. The premises were so over-heated that the eight nuns found it difficult to sleep. They awakened next morning to a snow-covered townscape. During World War Two, St. Margaret's became home, first to Polish soldiers (did any stay to marry in Paisley?) and then to members of the Royal Air Force.

The Society has been in two other locations since coming to Paisley; at Netherhill House, in Renfrew Road - a new school, occupied in 1922, was built in the convent grounds - and presently in Riccartsbar Avenue, where it has been since 1978. A postcard with an interesting message was sent, by Nannie MacDougal, from the Convent in 1906. 'We have three weeks holiday just now on account of diptheria which has broken in Paisley'. A report in the *Gazette* (dated 3rd November, two days before the postcard was posted) stated that '... only 29 cases were notified, as compared with 76 in the previous week. So far this week there are only 9 cases recorded'.

I can find no reference to this beauty spot in the Gleniffer Braes in any of my books. A linn (or lynn) is a waterfall. Views of the Linn are usually taken in summer and little can be done to achieve variety, but a scene in winter is more imaginative and dramatic and transforms the aspect of a subject. Does anyone know where 'Craigie' derives from?

This is an unusual and attractive view of the splendid building, showing the south elevation and revealing further facets of Honeyman's reassuring and inspired design. The Observatory is the home of active astronomical and space organisations and the 10 inch telescope may be used by the public. I recall that my wife and I decided to go along when Halley's Comet was visible (1985-6). We stopped to have a bag of chips and by the time our turn came to view, the comet had disappeared behind clouds.

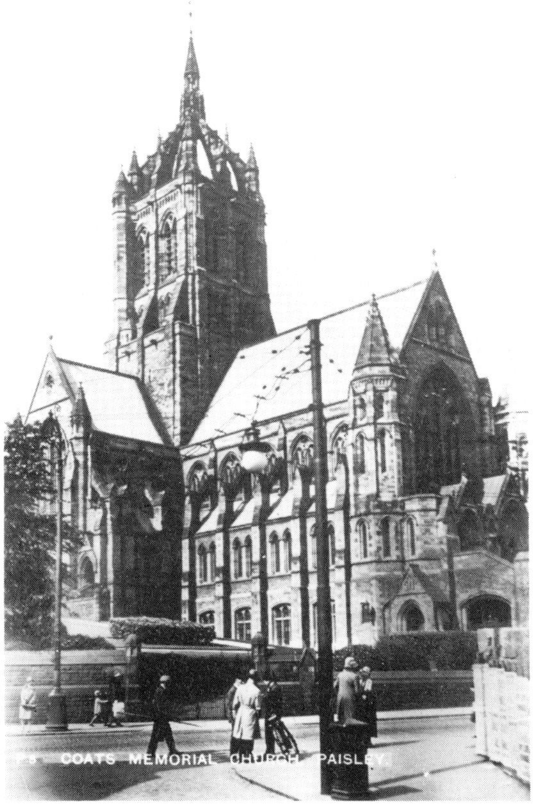

Few men or women have such a spectacular tribute paid to their memory as the building of this church, towering 240 feet into space, making it one of the largest non-conformist edifices in Europe. Hippolyte J. Blanc, a French architect, won the commission from six entries. Work began in 1885 and the church opened in May 1894, eleven years after the death of Thomas Coats. As far as is known, there were no fatalities during the construction of the church.

The University of Paisley now occupies the site of this reservoir. This was once the site of a muslin factory and the water was used for washing the raw materials and cloth. It was fed by a rivulet from Castlehead, which had been cut by the canal and ran off to St. Mirren's burn. The building on the right is probably part of the muslin factory. The original College building in George Street is on the site of the factory. My thanks to Dr. Sylvia Clark for these details.

This card is cleverly designed with the artist's name, W. Worsley, scratched in the plaster. It, like the three cards on the facing page, was a general issue available all over the country, but overprinted with local names. The verse on the card of the caricatured woman might puzzle some readers, so here's a translation: "I am not made of half pennies you pimple-faced, bulging-eyed image of half boiled porridge! I am just a poor lone person from Paisley!" (Note: there is no truth in the scurrilous rumour that the last sentence refers to the rump of the Labour Party after the next local elections.)

You are
always welcome at
PAISLEY

"AW'M NA' MADE O' BAWBEES YE PLOOKIE-FACIT, GOGGLE-E'ED IMAGE O' HAUF-BILIT PARRITCH! AW'M JEST A PUIR LONE BODY FRAE PAISLEY!"
The Wrench Series, No. 1026 (Copyright).

Everybody's
doing it
at Paisley

I wandered up and down this street in late September and came to the conclusion that it's much more interesting the higher you look. Towers, turrets, cupolas, balustrades, what I think are crow-stepped gables, pagodas and there might be a minaret or two; everywhere, harmony in stone. That's how a layman sees it. Walker, as always, describes it succinctly in clear architectural terms. Causeyside Street - the road from Kilmarnock (Clark) - dates from the early 18th Century and the name derives from the granite setts, or causeys, with which it was paved.

When the roads in Paisley were re-paved, loads of setts were sold off to find many uses in local gardens. This scene shows the imperial-looking facade of the Co-op. The street beyond there to Dunn Square has been re-developed. The cart on the left belonged to Walker, Dryborough & Co. who owned the Arkleston Print Works. The picture on the facing page shows upper Causeyside in the early 1930s.

In this scene from the 1920s, a house in which I stayed can be seen above the shop with the sun canopy. The building was replaced by a Galbraith's store, which, in turn, has given way to an Indian restaurant. This area has been reviving with renovation and construction taking place.

This scene has the John Neilson Institution dominating the skyline. The butcher's shop and other buildings on the right have been demolished to make way for the Co-op.

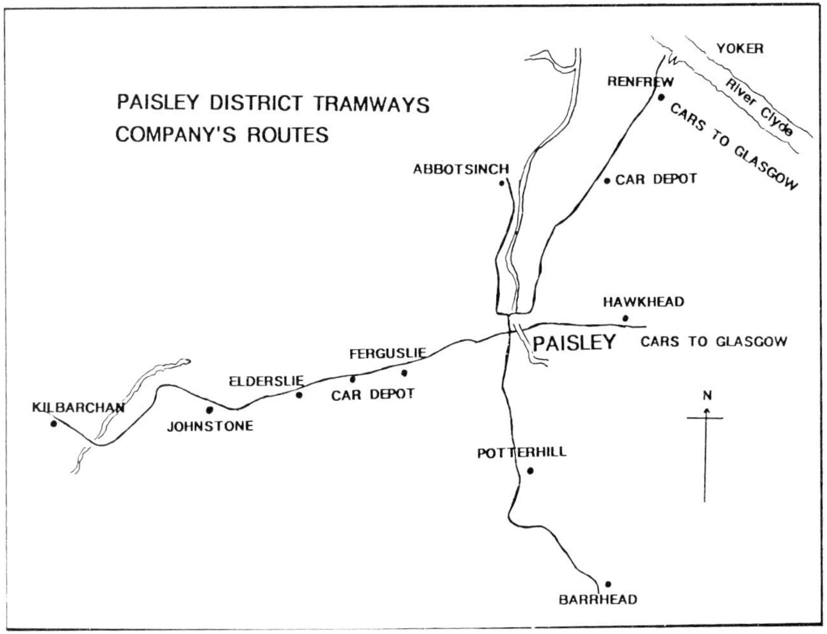

The Paisley Tramway Co. Ltd was incorporated in December 1884 and the first track was opened a year later. This ran from Garthland Place (where the Cathedral is located) to Broomlands. 'At the 1:19 gradient up to the Cross the Board of Trade Inspector, Major-General Hutchinson, stipulated that cars were not to exceed walking pace.' (Grieves). About fifty years before, John Scott Russell started a steam coach service, but a fatal accident ensure that horse-drawn cars reigned supreme until they were replaced by electric cars in 1904. The story of this episode in Paisley's transport is a fascinating one in which a certain William Martin Murphy, Chairman of the Dublin United Tramway Co. took on Paisley Town Council. It was an away win ... Read all about it in Grieve's book on the trams, volume one.

In 1907, the Tramway Company issued a set of twelve postcards in an attractive envelope. Frank Coutts, brother of the Tramway manager, was the artist. The night scene on the envelope shows a tram on its way to Kilbarchan.

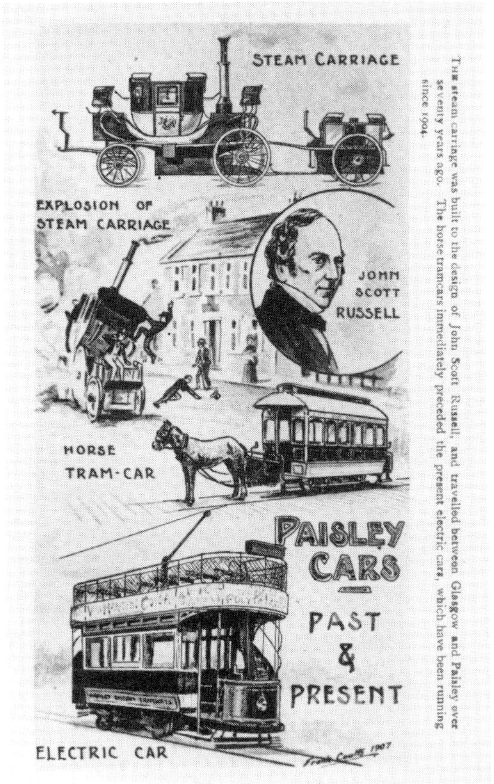

About three months after Russell's steam carriage started running, there was a boiler explosion outside the Halfway House, which killed four people. The first card traces the story from steam power in 1834 to electric trams in 1904. Paisley's last tram ran on 12th May 1957.

Card two shows some of the landmarks that could be reached by tram in and around Paisley. 'Crookston is most easily reached from Hawkhead, the others from the Potterhill and Barrhead route'. Each card had a skeletal route map on the back.

Considering that the set was issued to publicise the Tramway Company, the cards are disappointing, as only two actually feature trams. This splendid view showing the Walt Disney Town Hall features tram 42 on its way to Renfrew Ferry. The other Renfrew card in the set shows the ferry chuntering across to Yoker.

Initially, Potterhill was one of several agricultural villages in the area, just as there were weaving and mining villages. Evidence of that activity is lost as the land is now covered with houses. The left side of the road in this picture has been built on. A right turn at the bottom of the road (which leads to Barrhead) takes you to Glenburn. Potterhill was once a terminus of the tram route.

This picture is rather misleading, as the road to the Glen is not shown. What we see is, on the left, Potterhill and in the distance to the right, Thornly Park. Note the single track tram line. There are now houses on the left side all the way up to the corner of the road to the Glen. Running west from the junction is a row of older houses, originally built for managers and senior staff working at Fulton of the Glen. For most local people, the Glen meant either the works or the area of natural beauty. The Glen road now leads to Glenburn.

This suburb - 'three parallel roads of bourgeois villaland' (Walker) - is on the east side of Neilston Road and considerable new building has been going on in recent years. Construction began in the 1900s.

After passing through various owners, Glen House became the home of the Fulton family. William Fulton of Glenfield head of a famous Paisley bleaching firm, known familiarly as Fulton's of the Glen, was probably the most famous occupant. As with many Paisley landmarks, the house and the firm are long gone. The famous Glen or Tannahill Concerts were held on William Fulton's land. Just to the right of this picture were Stanley Dam and Castle.

This attractive little lodge or gate house stood at the entrance off the Glasgow Road. Note the bare trees and sprinkling of snow - and also what looks like some washing on the line at the right. It is difficult to date this picture (the postcard was sent in August 1915), but I suspect the publishers, Holmes, have doctored the background by removing houses, for surely there were buildings across the road. The clouds don't look real either. Perhaps local residents can provide some answers.

The gardens of Barshaw House became a public park in 1912 and this photograph dates from that time. According to Valerie Reilly, parts of the house date from the early 19th Century and were built by a Robert Smith. As we see it today, the building owes its appearance to a Glasgow merchant, James Arthur. Barshaw House was a military hospital in World War One. Many such houses were converted to that use. It was a maternity unit in 1958, as our elder son was born there. In a way, it has now come full circle in its utilisation as a geriatric hospital.

Paisley is well-endowed with parks. Brodie Park resulted from a bequest by the late Robert Brodie in 1871 of 26 acres including his house, in the south side of town. The park was officially opened in May 1877. This view has much of interest such as the attractive cast iron fountain. But the main interest lies in the houses in the background, a rare form of tenement called 'double-drum', in Carriagehill. The turretted house at the right is on the corner with Brodie Park Avenue.

The Widow and Granddaughter of Robert Burns.

Mrs Burns (Jean Armour) and one of her Grandchildren (a daughter of Captain James Glencairn Burns of the East India Company's Service).

Jean Armour was born 1765 and married the poet in 1788, whom she survived 38 years. She died in 1834 in her 70th year.

Left: The poet's statue in the Fountain Gardens. In the background is the tenement on the corner of Caledonia Street and MacDowell Street - still there. The chimneys behind the houses are gone, although MacDowell Street is still an industrial area, as it has been for most of its existence. The design of the Burns statue, by F.W. Pomeroy (not S.W. as printed in volume one), is not unique. Peter Westwood, Publicity Officer for the Burns Federation, tells me that there are two others, one in Sydney, Australia and the other in Auckland, New Zealand.

Right: In March 1786, Jean Armour of Mauchline was pregnant by Robert Burns. Her father, James Armour, wanted nothing to do with Burns who was at that time unknown. Jean was sent to Paisley. There she lodged with Andrew Purdie, a carpenter, in the Old Sneddon. A prospective suitor in Paisley was Robert Wilson, a weaver, but it came to nothing and Jean eventually returned to Mauchline, where she had twins on 17th October 1786. A year later, she was again pregnant by Burns. However, he had meanwhile published the Kilmarnock Edition of his poems and was thus now acceptable to James Armour. They married in 1788. On 12th September, he wrote to her from Ellisland: 'My dear Love, I received your kind letter with a pleasure which no letter but one from you could have given me, - I dreamed of you the whole night last'... How the words wing across the years and tug at the heart.

This scene can be dated to within a few months of tram 1050 entering service in April 1924. The Cenotaph was officially unveiled on the 27th of July that year. The tram was designed by Sir John James Burnet (who designed many notable buildings in Glasgow including the Alhambra Theatre) and was at the time of this picture, painted blue. In the wake of the tram car are some of the buses which eventually killed the tram off including one from Fullars of Paisley.

'The most glorious work of modern days in the Methodism of Scotland' That was how the Reverend J. Williams Butcher, Chairman of the Scotland District of the Wesleyan Methodist Church, described the events culminating in the opening of the hall in 1908. John Wesley paid the last of his 22 visits to Scotland when he was 87, but it seems that passing through the town en route from Glasgow to Greenock was as near as he got to Paisley. Although there were about forty Methodists in Paisley in 1806, it was with the coming of English navigators (navvies) to start building the canal in 1807 that Methodism became firmly established. The first regular meeting-place was built in George Street, in 1810, when a regular core of about 125 members contributed towards the cost. From 1810 until 1908 they met in various places in the town.

Shown on these cards, used in 1909/10, are John Slack (left) and the Rev W.H. Rolls. Slack had passed his time as a gambler, racehorse owner, entertainer and dedicated drinker until he was converted to Christianity by Joseph Nix (the Racecourse Preacher) and Rolls. That was in 1904 and he was a bright flame for Methodism until his death in 1909. Rolls was prevailed upon to take up the ministry in Paisley and did so until his death in 1910.

Charles Glasgow built two models of State coaches, which he completed in 1932 after three years' work. The vehicle in this picture shows His Majesty the King's Semi State Coach. Mr Glasgow spent many weeks at the Royal Mews sketching, measuring and photographing. Their Majesties commented favourably on the meticulous detail of the models.

The Daily Mail Circuit of Britain Air Race of July 1911 was one of the great pioneer aviation races, covering 1,010 miles, Brooklands to Brooklands. Paisley was the third official Scottish control point, at St. James' Park, the Racecourse (although the official programme lists Glasgow and not Paisley); the others were at Edinburgh and Stirling. Five pilots reached the Racecourse. Beaumont (the eventual winner), Vedrines (25th) and Hamel (26th) took off within an hour of landing. Valentine arrived just after 8 o'clock on the 26th and visited the Kibble Reformatory where '... the little urchins ... had stolen from their beds at the unwanted sound, and each window in the dormitory was crowded by eager-eyed and interested spectators'. He stayed overnight at the Globe Hotel in the High Street and took off at 11.55 the next day. Cody landed on the 29th and, as the race was already over, spent a leisurely two days in the town, accepting Mr. Love's hospitality at the Kibble. This picture shows Valentine and was given to me by the late Mr William Adam, of Johnstone, who was in the crowd with his father.

You can't get much more close-up than this, with an 'imperious conductor and motorman', as they were characterised by a correspondent in 1906. He did add that they were 'so well dressed', giving a sort of naval effect. Anyone who received a broadside from an irate conductor will know what he meant. 1050 was re-built in May 1930 and emerged, like a butterfly, in yellow. She clanged her last clang in June 1960. The picture was probably taken at Potterhill. I have a postcard with the message, "we have the electric cars running from Glasgow through Paisley and right into Johnston; also up to Potterhill".

Another superb photograph, from 1905. The open-top tramcar was heading for Renfrew Ferry. The church on the left is the Martyr's Parish. I wonder why the young girl on the right didn't turn towards the camera. She must have been curious to know what the other people were looking at! The picture shows graphically how comparatively narrow the street was before the old tenements on the right were demolished and replaced by tenements built behind them.

‘Gordon Street, on the South side of the town, was once the main bus route to the Coast. At the top of the street, where it meets Causeyside Street, was the depot for Young’s Buses. The pend is still there, on the left. Almost every Sunday during the summer, my parents and I joined the throngs of people going on the many tours on offer. Also in Gordon Street was the premisies of printers and publishers James Paton, seen on the right of the card, proprietors of the Paisley Gazette.’

This scene, looking roughly north-west, dates to before 1923. Part of the vast open space at the right became the Anchor Recreation Ground, for the use of mill employees, and Abercrombie and Maitland's back-to-back pavilion is nowhere in sight. The dark ribbon running through the picture is the river, passing in front of the Finishing Mill, at left centre. The river can be seen wending towards the town via the hammills and the Town Hall and the Abbey are faintly discernible. Much of the foreground is now lost under housing. The ice rink and swimming pool have taken a piece out of Seedhill Park, at the middle of the scene.

The first steam-powered thread mills in Paisley belonged to William and James Carlile of New Sneddon. The second was opened by James Clark, at Seedhill, in 1812. His sons and one of the Kerr family were associated with the firm. They made the first machine-spun cotton, which was soon in demand as sewing thread. The thread was on spools, not in hanks, another innovation. (Hands up those of you who remember buying a bag of bobbins as kindling?) Burnside Mill was built in 1858, the same time as the iron girder bridge, still there, but gradually disappearing behind a profusion of weeds and wild flowers. The Atlantic and the Pacific Mills were built in the 1860s and 1870s and George Aitken Clark set the machinery in motion at the Atlantic in 1872. The Finishing Mill (illustrated above) dates from 1886 and the Mile End Mill from 1899-1900.

Most of the design was by Woodhouse and Morley of Bradford, who were responsible for the Ferguslie thread empire. Coats effectively took over Clark's, together with various English companies, in 1896; *Anchor* (Clark) was firmly welded to *Chain* (Coats).

The picture on the opposite page shows the Finishing Mill, with the Saucel Distillery in the centre of the picture. All the other buildings have gone. The view on this page is substantially the same, taken after 1911, when the fire escapes were added to the Finishing Mill. Note the building with the 'X'. The message on the back of the postcard, sent in 1929, reads: 'The place marked X is Mrs Craig the Cart runs through the garden. Have been to the "Talkies" they are great'. This postcard is a re-issue of an older one - an abandoned pram has been touched out of the picture!

An evocative view, looking towards the Finishing Mill. Not so evocative is the amount of pollution in the river from the industries along its banks. The iron bridge can just be discerned. The factory at the right might be part of the Anchor Mills complex or possibly they are bleaching sheds.

'The architects of this splendid building, The Finishing Mill, were Woodhouse and Morley of Bradford. It dates from 1886; the James Calentine code number, 21995 J.V. indicates a publication date of the picture as 1894. The card dates from the early 1900's. It appears that the building is now going to be renovated to accommodate a supermarket, flats, offices and a Coats Museum. Given its spectacular site on the River Cart, with a myriad lights, it will resemble an ocean liner at anchor (appropriately!) and will enhance the area.'

One of a set of six distorted view postcards of the town.

The area was a natural site for mills. Pollution though, both natural and industrial, became such a problem that it was suggested in 1856 that this outcrop of rock (the Hamills) be blown up to ease the passage of the water and its contents. This atmospheric photo shows to the right what is now The Watermill (with other buildings since demolished) and centre, the Saucel Distillery. Imagine Frankenstein wading across here on a stormy day, on his way to complain about his council tax..

J & P Coats' Football Team 1922-23. I am not sure but am assuming they were a Paisley team, given the strong Coats presence in the town (soon to be no more, as the remnant of this once-great empire is removing to some obscure village). The people shown here are (from left to right):
Front row: Gallagher, Robertson (Trainer), Morley, Neilsen, Gilmour, Fleming. Second row: Lappin, Stevenson, McIntosh, McAvoy, Douglas (Trainer). Third row: John Walmsley (President), Schofield, Ferguson. Back row: E. Bowe (Chairman), George Morley (Asst. Manager), Harry Wade (Manager), Joseph Tennyson (Treasurer).

I sneaked this one in while the publisher wasn't looking. Ostensibly of Dunn Square, it's the background that makes it interesting. Behind the white building in the centre is part of the prison. At the right is the south wall of the Theatre. The front faced east, on to Smithhills. There was already a Bank Street Theatre when in 1825 another was set up in a half-ruined building in New Smithhills, which would be the site of the new theatre. The great Edmund Kean acted *Richard III* in the Smithhills Street Theatre in September 1827. Other famous names to appear there were Chaplin and Pavlova. The Logan Family were regular performers. Just prior to demolition, Philip Doughty (of Frank Hardy Studios) was commissioned to photograph the theatre and other buildings and he suggested that I formed part of the scene - I just happened to be passing at the time. But I didn't.

The growth of towns over the centuries is always fascinating and Paisley's expansion was such that, by 1946, when the Housing Act permitted a widening of its boundaries, the burgh became the largest in Scotland, ten times the size of its mediaeval counterpart. Hunterhill was one of the three council estates to commence building then. Running along the foot of the picture is Barrhead Road, while at the right is the gatehouse of Hawkhead House. A nursery now occupies the area. The prefabs, meant to be temporary buildings, got a facelift some years ago and are in fine fettle.

Falside Road runs west from the road to Barrhead. Opposite the houses is a supermarket, this side of the former Brown & Polson factory, still in business under a new name. The house at the left is the only one still there today, although the railings have gone. It was built around 1851 and the windows downstairs were altered in the early 1900s. At 29 Falside, in July 1913, there was a murder and a suicide. The *Gazette* of 5th July commented: 'Paisley has been remarkably free from serious crime for many years and, needless to add, Wednesday evening's tragedy has been the chief topic in the town during the week'. The wife was buried in Hawkhead, while her husband found his last resting-place at the Thorn Cemetery, Johnstone.

1872 was a benchmark year in education with the Bill brought in by the Lord Advocate (Young) being accepted and receiving the Royal assent. Every burgh was required to have a School Board, each to comprise nine members. Each householder paying £4 or more annually in rent had nine votes to be distributed as he or she pleased. Of the nine selected, the runaway winner was Mrs Arthur of Barshaw with 6293 votes, but inevitably Mr Thomas Coats was elected chairman. He donated £1000 each towards the construction of four schools at the cardinal points of the town and all were opened by 9th September 1876. Another school quickly became necessary and Craigielea/Ferguslie was opened in McKenzie Street on 4th September 1882. It was closed in 1974, suffered vandalism and burning and the shell was demolished in 1978.

The Institute was gifted to the town by Miss Agnes Russell, of Muirfield, Castlehead, as a memorial to her brothers Robert and Thomas (R & T Russell, Solicitors). It was opened officially by HRH Princess Mary, the Princess Royal in March 1927, as a clinic for children and is still in use today. Construction began in 1924, by such well-known local firms as Lang (joinery) and Kilpatrick (electrical). The architect was Paisley man J. Steel Maitland, with the figures sculpted by Archibald Dawson. The skeleton fabric was of reinforced concrete, the first of its kind in the West of Scotland. The Dean of Guild, passing the plans in 1923, apparently queried the cost of the building - I suppose that bureaucrats are born to meddle - but no-one ever got to know the final total. Good for Miss Russell!

According to McCarthy, '...the new streets of Saint James, Glen and Caledonia were laid out and the area built up before 1830'. The street runs west, with the Holy Trinity Church at the east end and the Sheriff Court at the left. Moncrieff the fishmongers was under the awning and just this side of the awning, through the pend, was a garage. The yard on the right belonged to McConnell (builders) and A.M. Pottie had a garage and showroom farther along the street. Demolition and re-building have altered the appearance of the scene on the right and, of course, the granite setts have gone. For a time in the 1950s and 1960s, bus services used St. James Street as a terminus and I can remember Paton's of Renfrew Ferry and McGill's of Barrhead.

On the right all the houses and shops as far as this side of the Fountain Gardens have been demolished and replaced by new housing. There have also been considerable changes on the left - the street runs north, from the west end of St. James - and I took photographs of McKean's Starch Works smoking giant being laid low. At the end of Caledonia Street, at its junction with three other roads, lies Love Street, the lair of St. Mirren. I stayed twice in Caledonia Street, first of all in No.47. We had no bathrooms and I had my dips in the big copper boiler in the wash-house. My other house was round the corner from Glen Street. As it has been demolished, I guess that a grateful Council will stick up my plaque at 47.... During the Clydebank Blitz, we used to sit and listen to the Heinkels and the Spitfires roaring up the street and in the mornings I would go out and pick up shrapnel.

A scene from the first decade of the century. The tramcar is going to Kilbarchan and is probably no.42. The tea and coffee warehouse on the right was demolished in the 1920s. Running off to the right is Moss Street.

A marvellous scene, dating from the 1920s, I think. The facade of the Town Hall stands out clearly. Through the gap can be seen part of the Abbey Mill and the tramcar, passing the Paisley Savings Bank, is probably headed for Potter-hill. The car (HS 842) is negotiating a tricky passage past the women with the pram, who seem unconcerned by its proximity.

Issued as a scene of Dunn Square, to Paisley-watchers this postcard view is far more interesting for its other aspects, particularly that magnificent parade of buildings drawn up for inspection on the west side of the street dating from around 1872-77. Paisley's third empire, that of the Paisley Co-operative Manufacturing Society, begins at the foot of the brae. Construction of this swathe of tenements stretches from the early 19th century till 1932. The buildings demand 'Look at us, don't just walk past'. So go and look! The transport in this scene is also fascinating: Morris Minor, Morris Traveller, Ford Popular, Austin Seven and a GPO van at work.

This photo probably dates to 1908, the year that the YMCA was opened. The legend J. DOUGLAS RITCHIE PHOTOGRAPHER can still be seen above the top windows of the YMCA building and my wife worked there. No less a personality than the famous photographer George Edward Russell, in his studio on the upper floors, had his patience strained to the limit, trying to get our younger lad to sit up and pose for his portrait. I think that G.E.R. retired shortly after that episode.

A SELECT BIBLIOGRAPHY

Brotchie A.W. and Grieves R.L.	Paisley's Trams and Buses: 2 volumes: Eighties to Twenties, 1986 Twenties to Eighties, 1988; N.B. Traction, Dundee
Burgess, Moira	Discover Paisley: 1991; Department of Arts Libraries, Renfrew District Council
Clark, Sylvia	Paisley: a History; 1988; Mainstream Publishing
Kirk, Brian R.	Thomas Coats Memorial Church; 1992; published by the Church
Leitch, Archie	Paisley Methodist Central Hall; 1983; published by the Hall
McAlpine, C. Joan	Barshaw and the Arthurs; 1989; private publication?
McCarthy, Mary	A Social Geography of Paisley; 1969; Paisley Public Library
Malcolm, Donald	Cody and the Great Air Race; 1978; Renfrew District Libraries
Malcolm, Donald	Yesterday's Paisley; 1991; Richard Stenlake Publishing
Malden, John	Let Paisley Flourish; 1991; Museum & Art Galleries, Paisley
Moodie, Leslie H.	When Lighting Struck Paisley; no date, no published noted My copy was bought in 1988.
Reilly, Valerie	Paisley in Old Picture Postcards; 1983; European Library
Rowand, David	The Pictorial History of Paisley; 1992; Alloway Publishing
Walker, Frank Arneil	The South Clyde Estuary; 1986; Scottish Academic Press
Paisley Diocese	The Faithful Companions of Jesus, 1889-1989
Local History Department, Renfrew District Libraries	The Russell Institute; 1981

Had the finance been available, the tower of the clock at Charleston (1887) would have been constructed in stone for £300. In agreement with the owner of the building, the Property Committee (of the Council) sanctioned a tower of pitch pine, 'not to cost more than £200'. The flat-topped ogee dome is an attractive feature on the gaudily-painted courtesan of a tower. The four, six-foot clock faces and mechanism were installed by Duff and Millar; opal glass was utilised and the lighting was automatic. However, things did not tick over smoothly. It was discovered that the tower was letting in water, eventually traced to the vibration of the mechanism.